This book belongs to:

Leos Gallery

My Dream

Hi! My name is Leo. I'd like to tell you my story, as I heard something bad happened to you and that you are feeling sad. I'm a grown up now, but I remember very well what it was like being a child. I used to spend a lot of time drawing and I kept some of the pictures that I made back then.

Now that I am a professional artist, I selected, restored and hung a few of my old drawings in the back of my shop. I hope they cheer you up, at least a bit. They sometimes tell a sad story, but they will lead to a happy ending, I promise. I will tell you what happened to me, so you can learn a few things that I would have wanted to know back when I was your age. I, for example, know now that being sad is part of growing up.

But, let's start at the beginning. First, I'll tell you about my experience and then I'll explain what helped me to feel happy again.

Beginnings

I grew up in Germany and started drawing one day after going on a shopping trip with my parents and my little sister, Kiki. In the pedestrian zone of the shopping area, an older man was sitting on a bench and sketching. I stopped, while the others in my family kept on walking. My mum got annoyed as I had suddenly disappeared and they had to search for me. However, I couldn't stop watching the man's nimble fingers. Starting with a blank sheet of white paper, he drew thin lines, then darker areas, and step by step a beautiful fountain appeared. I knew right then that I wanted to learn that craft.

As soon as we got home that day, I ran to my room, sat down at my desk, took the pencils from my drawer and started drawing. Even though, at that time, I wasn't very good, I showed the drawing to my mum and she told me that I had done really well for my first attempt. She then explained that I needed to practice more if I wanted to become an artist. Suddenly, I knew what I wanted to be in life.

Water Battle

From that moment on, I started using my pencils more and began drawing on a daily basis. Sometimes it was just for a few minutes, sometimes for the whole afternoon. My mum always told me that my drawings were beautiful and that I would get even better the more I practiced. If I needed pens or paper, we would go together to buy some at the art shop nearby where there were drawings on display and you could buy every kind of art supply you can imagine. I didn't know what most of them were for, but I knew that one day, I wanted to own a store like that.

One hot summer's day, while my sister was fooling around with a water gun, she sprayed Dad. He then pulled Mum into the spray and within minutes, the whole family was having a water fight. I threw a big bucket of cold water over Kiki. I never heard her scream that loud ever again. I laughed and laughed. It was so nice! At the end of that great day, I drew a picture for my mum of the fun we had had. I called it "Water Battle" and she said it was her favourite drawing. After making that picture, I noticed how soothing it was to draw before going to bed. I still do that.

Finn and I

One day, a new kid called Finn moved to our neighbourhood and started at my school. He was placed in my class and we hung out together almost every day. Even as grown-ups, we still meet up all the time. He didn't like to draw, but he loved football and was the best goalkeeper in school. After doing our homework, we would go exploring on our bikes, searching for dinosaur traces in the forest or building traps to catch squirrels, as we wanted to pet them. Sometimes we played video games or tricks on Kiki.

I didn't like my little sister when we were children. We argued a lot and got angry with each other multiple times a day. She always wanted to sit at my desk and use my pencils, which was annoying. Finn lent me a whoopee cushion and I would slip it under Kiki's bottom every once in a while and call her 'fart face' for weeks!

That One
Moment

I can tell you the exact moment I noticed that something was wrong with my mum. She had been coughing a lot and needing to rest often, but I didn't think it was such a big deal. I only knew that something serious was up when I overheard my parents talking in the living room one night. I should have been sleeping, but I was thirsty and on my way to the kitchen. I had barely walked past the living room door when I heard my dad sobbing. I had never heard him like that before.

I stopped and got scared. However, since I wasn't sure what to do, I quietly went back to bed. But I couldn't sleep. I stayed awake for hours thinking what I had heard. I never told anyone about it. I hardly talked to Kiki anyway, as she always wanted to draw with chalk on my desk and subsequently destroyed my pictures.

By the way, if you're wondering what was wrong with my mum, she had a very rare disease. So rare, in fact, it doesn't actually exist.

White Turns Red

The day came when Mum had to go into hospital. She packed her bag the night before, while we were chatting about school. She always held a tissue in her hand, as she was permanently coughing and using it to cover her mouth. I noticed that the white tissue had turned red, but I didn't dare ask why. Still, Mum noticed my worried expression and told me that the doctors would help her to get well again.

She spent some time in hospital, perhaps a few days. I can't remember exactly anymore. We were allowed to visit her, but the time at the hospital was always very boring. When Mum returned home, she was thinner and her eyes didn't shine as bright as they had before. She also spoke slower and quieter. Yet, I was sure things would get better. Meanwhile, I tried to cause as little trouble as possible so she could rest. Kiki continued trying to come into my room, but now she only took a step or two before I chased her away. However, when I was not in my room, she snuck in and broke my pencils. In retaliation, I hid her toys.

At the Zoo

Over the following weeks and months, Mum got a bit weaker every day. Her hair began to fall out, so she started wearing a headscarf most of the time. One day, we went to the zoo, but I didn't realise then that it would be our last trip together. I remember her walking in front of me and somehow knowing that something bad was going to happen. She no longer looked like my mum, but more like a shadow of herself. Whilst walking around, she had to sit and take a break at every bench we passed and would begin breathing heavily again after just a few steps. Nevertheless, she still smiled, she always did, and I hold on to that memory.

That whole experience was new to me. I somehow felt nothing and yet everything simultaneously. I was overwhelmed and also helpless, as I had no idea how to deal with such a situation. But I learned that everybody feels like that sometimes and that's okay. Time will pass and things will be better. However, sometimes, when I was not in a good mood, I took it out on Kiki, playing tricks on her over and over again. At the zoo, for example, because she was afraid of the donkeys and only dared to observe them from a distance, I snuck up behind her and pushed her near them. One donkey then pulled her hat off and she ran away screaming. I laughed so hard, but only until Dad caught me.

One Night

A few days later, I woke up in the middle of the night. All the lights in the house were on and Dad was walking up and down the hallway, talking frantically on the phone. When he saw me, he told me everything would be fine and shooed me back to my room. Kiki's door was closed. I went back to bed but tossed and turned, trying to get back to sleep. Then, from my window, I saw the street suddenly become illuminated by a flashing blue light. I jumped out of bed and looked outside. The lights hissed past my window and stopped by our garden gate. My heart missed a beat. In an instant, two men carrying cases jumped out of the ambulance and ran to our front door.

I opened my bedroom door a crack and peeked out. The men in red uniforms were hurrying through the hallway, past my door, to my parents' bedroom. Then Dad came to my room carrying Kiki. He explained that Grandma was coming over, that Mum was not doing well, but the doctors were taking care of her. I believed that Mum would be fine. After all, she was my mum. It was crystal clear she would get well again. It couldn't be any other way.

Kiki and I were sitting in the living room when the men carried Mum on a stretcher to the front door. Seeing her, otherwise strong and in a good mood, suddenly so helpless, was like a slap in the face that hurt deeply. The worst part was that there was nothing I could do except stand by and watch. But, from time to time, there simply are situations like this, which, thankfully, are very rare. My sister told me years later that for some it's comforting just to have someone nearby.

Hospital

The next day, Dad, Kiki and I visited Mum in hospital. The sun was shining, but Mum could hardly get out of bed. When she asked for some fresh air, Dad opened the window. He then left the room and Mum told Kiki and me to lie on the bed next to her. We just lay there for a while not saying a word – that felt good. Mum hugged us and told us that she was happy to have two such awesome children. That was one of the last things my mum said to me and I am happy about that.

Incidentally, I believe that all mums and dads would say something like that, but only some have the opportunity. I only realized a lot later how lucky Kiki and I were. We had a chance to talk to Mum one last time. Dad told me years later that her heart had stopped beating in the ambulance, but the two men had managed to resuscitate her – to bring her back to life. I think she wanted to say goodbye to us and fought to stay alive for a little longer. It took me a long time, but now I am very grateful for that afternoon and for the actions of the paramedics. I still remember and often think back to the minutes we spent in that weird-smelling bed.

At
Grandma's

Later that evening, Dad dropped us off at Grandma's and went back to the hospital. That was the night my mum went into a sleep so deep that nobody could wake her. Kiki kept following me around Grandma's house, asking if I knew what was going on. However, I was angry because I had wanted to stay with Mum but was not allowed to. In my mood, I threw my pencils on the floor and shouted at Kiki, telling her to shut up because it was obvious what was happening.

She stared at me, startled and ran to Grandma crying. For some time, she didn't ask me anything. I had no idea what was going on for her. Now I know that she was even more scared than I was. That was the first evening I didn't want to draw. Instead, I wanted to rest and watch TV. I spent most of the night awake in bed, wallowing, until I could no longer keep my eyes open.

· Only in Bed ·

The next morning, Grandma woke me with tears in her eyes and told me that Mum had stopped breathing during the night. I had somehow known that I would hear those words, but had no idea how powerful they would be. Within a moment I felt like someone had wrapped me in a hundred towels and sat on them. I could hardly breathe. The world was somehow quiet and the only response I could give was to shake my head. With tears rolling down her face, Grandma hugged me tightly. I felt petrified. She then had to go to Kiki and left me alone.

I stopped talking, hardly ate anything and wanted to be alone. I felt nothing, empty inside. My happiness and any desire to do anything had vanished. The telephone at our house didn't stop ringing that day. So, while I just lay in bed, Dad was busy answering the calls and making arrangements. He hardly took a break and this annoyed me, as I really needed him at that time. While lying motionless in my bed, I noticed a ladybird on my windowsill. Mum had told us several times that they were her favourite insect as they brought good luck. However, because I was feeling so angry, I wanted to kill it. Fortunately, I was too weak to even get out of bed and just left it alone.

The Funeral

I hated the day of the funeral. Everyone was crying, including Dad. Even though he was usually very composed among other people. I couldn't cry. Instead, I stood there feeling lost. Kiki was next to me. People shook our hands and said something. We had never experienced anything like it. Everyone was dressed in black and stared at the floor the whole time. Even my uncle, who usually told jokes, cried and said nothing. I didn't know how I felt – kind of angry, but lacking the strength to make it noticeable. I was just there among all the others, but like I didn't belong.

During the funeral I kept looking at Finn and saw tears in his eyes. As silly as it sounds, that helped me – knowing that he also felt sad was somehow comforting. It was only after the ceremony, when only the three of us got in the car, that I realised what had happened. Then I started crying. It was unfair. There were so many bad people who were allowed to still be in this world, but my mum, who had always been good to everyone, had to die. It didn't make sense. It didn't for a long time.

I drew the picture of the funeral a lot later. I wanted to draw it earlier, but I couldn't. I wasn't ready. But that's okay. We are only ready when we are ready.

Black

The day after the funeral, the house was dipped in silence and somehow my insides were too. Everything looked the same, but felt different. By the evening, after sitting silently in my room all afternoon, I wanted to draw something with my pencils. As soon as I grabbed them, they reminded me of Mum and tears started rolling down my face. The paper got wet and I got angry because none of the pencils wanted to draw. So, one by one, I broke them all and threw them into the corner. It wasn't until I got to the black pencil that I thought I'd be able to do something with it. I used it over a large area and called the picture "Black", because that was the way I felt.

Right before bedtime, Dad came into my room with Kiki. I thought he would scold me for the mess I had made, but it didn't matter to him. Instead, we talked about what was going to change. He explained that we would now spend more time with Grandma. He promised that Mum was alright now, that she was proud of her children and would now take care of us from above. That was similar to what Grandma had told us. She believed that Mum was now an angel in heaven. I didn't want to hear any of it. I wanted her to be alive again. Nothing else could help me in that moment.

The Empty
Chair

Subsequently, everyday life resumed. But, somehow, it was no longer the everyday life I had known. I went back to school, but now Dad was packing the lunch boxes and they were very different – don't ask! I spent a lot of time with Finn, who kept fooling around, even though I wanted to be sad. After school, instead of Mum, Grandma was waiting for me when I came home. The worst part was having dinner at night, when one chair remained empty. We put a plate down for Mum for a while. That helped a little. I missed her so much and thought about her all the time. It was just so unfair.

All I had on my mind was what I could have done differently so Mum would have recovered. I could think of nothing else, but found no answer to my question. The only thing that helped, was to occupy my hands. If they were busy, I could switch off and let go for at least a little bit. In the end, I drew for days on end and got better and better. Nevertheless, I cried often; it felt liberating. After some time, I started to talk again – just a few words a day, but every day a few more. In retrospect, I learned that small steps will take you to a destination far away.

Change

After the funeral, it was hard to concentrate on my schoolwork. When it was quiet and I wanted to study, I only had Mum on my mind. Dad understood that I was trying, but not managing. Even when I almost had to repeat the year, he kept telling me it would be okay. He said that I could let things slide for a while, but the day had to come when I would feel like my old self again. I was so frustrated. I stopped drawing, hardly took part in any conversation and just kept to myself. That was the sad version of me and, at the same time, the new version of me. At least that's what I thought back then. I was sure I would stay like that forever. But, in reality, it was only a phase. I didn't realise then that the happy me was still inside me.

One night around that time, I heard Kiki open my bedroom door. She was standing in the dark snivelling. I don't think she dared to come to me until I said something. Then she crawled into my bed. I took her in my arms and comforted her as best I could. Then we cried together. We had never gotten along very well, but that night was like a fresh start. Over the next few weeks, months and years we became inseparable, and we still are today. From time to time, I still play tricks on her, but they are different from how they used to be.

Together

Months passed and I still missed Mum. I had gotten used to the new circumstances, but I never smiled. Nothing gave me pleasure. Dad kept telling me that I should continue to draw, but when I sat at my desk, nothing inspired me. One day, Dad said something that somehow awakened my ambition. "Draw a picture of your mother," he suggested. Suddenly, that was what I wanted to put on paper but, of course, it would have to be as perfect as possible. Subsequently, I spent a long time creating that one drawing and started over dozens of times, but the end result was never good enough. I got obsessed and practiced over and over. "Only with practice can you become an artist," Mum had told me. Now I worked harder than ever before.

Kiki was very attached to me at that time. She was always by my side, watching me draw or playing with her toys in my room. I think she just didn't want to be alone and needed someone. From time to time, I sat her at my desk and we drew together. I showed her some tricks and we had a laugh every now and then. That also distracted me from my thoughts.

One day, Kiki asked me to draw her a picture of Mum, too, but she wanted her to have wings. I did one of us sitting at my desk looking at Mum in the sky. That picture now hangs in Kiki's flat. My drawing of Mum hangs in my home. Both bring a smile to my face every time I see them.

At the
Grave

Whenever I missed Mum too much, I visited her at the cemetery. I usually took something to drink and sat down in the middle of her grave. I felt closer to her there. I told her everything that was going on – how things were going at school and what Finn and I had gotten up to. That helped a lot, because I truly said the things that I wanted to tell her, to my mum. If there was someone else in the cemetery, I didn't care. I just did what I thought was best for me. In my opinion, she heard my words, even if some people claim something else.

Sometimes, I took my drawings with me and showed them to her. Only rarely did I take Kiki, but she was always happy when we were with Mum. For my birthday that year, I got something that I had completely forgotten about: a clipboard, like the man at the fountain had used to draw on. I often sat in the cemetery and worked there. It was so nice and quiet and I could be undisturbed. I didn't notice back then, but the more time passed, the more colourful my drawings became again. One day, the gravedigger came over to me and explained that people don't usually sit in the middle of graves. I nodded and positioned myself on the gravel in front of the grave. To me, this was somehow a sign, because after that conversation I felt less sad.

Mashed
Frog's Legs

I cannot tell you an exact moment when things were better again. I just woke up one morning and although I still missed Mum, I also realised that my life was still beautiful. Somewhere along the way, I had accepted that I had to live my life without my Mum. Instead, I was much closer to Kiki, I could talk to Dad about anything and having Grandma nearby was also kind of nice. I still felt sad, but less frequently. Now, I think of Mum with joy and what happened to her is simply part of my life story. Something bad happens to everyone sometime, but it is important that you don't let it tear you down, that you keep your head up and look ahead. At some point, it will be better.

Later, I wanted to study art, but my grades weren't good enough, so I trained as a house painter. Back then, I thought that that would be the end of my artistic career. After all, I only painted walls. But, actually, that was just the beginning. I simply learned different things about paint, brushes and painting techniques. In the evening, I still drew and practiced or else I was with either Finn or Kiki. One time, my sister and I played a trick on Finn.

For days, I had been telling him that my dad was about to cook mashed frog's legs. Then, when the time was right, I talked Finn into eating the leftovers of our dinner. It looked like dad's culinary art, but, since he had learned how to cook, it actually tasted good. Then, as Finn was snacking on the leftovers, Kiki came into the kitchen, holding a frog. She then asked Finn if he was enjoying his frog's legs and told him that she had gotten some more. He suddenly remembered my frog tales and went dead silent. I almost burst with laughter. We then released the frog into the garden pond and named him Mario. He stayed with us throughout the summer.

Siblings

Cola

Over time, more and more people noticed my art and I was able to sell some pictures. It was still a long time until I had my own gallery, but it was worth the wait. Kiki helped me decorate and organise everything. As she had put on a lot of perfume that day, I secretly painted a few white lines down the back of her black shirt, called her the weirdest smelling 'Skunk' anyone had ever seen and imitated growling noises. I also set up my desk in the shop and usually paint there as it reminds me of Mum. Sometimes, I miss her, but I'm also happy how the rest of my life has turned out. When those things happened, I thought my life was over – that's what it felt like. But now I know that even the worst grief comes to an end. Incidentally, the pencils in my drawer were just the beginning. In due time, I expanded my skills, trying new painting materials, like acrylics and watercolours. I also tried different ways to express myself such as wood carving, but that wasn't for me.

Now you have seen all the drawings in my exhibition. I hope you liked them and that my story has helped you, at least a bit. By the way, I left two spaces free in my gallery, for you to contribute a picture, if you want. I am already excited to see your ideas. You can draw or paint whatever you want – whatever comes to mind, whatever wants to get out. It can be a picture of people, animals, things or experiences. It's entirely up to you.

Now, I'm going to leave you. I just came up with a new idea and I need to paint before it goes out of my mind! See you! Have fun!

More from the author:

Being happy with Nevis

The story of a butterfly may not seem wild,
but this tale was written to help every child.
Nevis dreams about getting out of his cocoon,
yet neither kicking nor screaming is helping soon.
That's how Nevis' story starts unhappily,
but then he notices, how happy he can be.

In the insect kingdom they promise,
that every human summons happiness,
if he only reads this book to kids
and then closes both eyelids.
Whether this is really true,
you decide, but only for you.

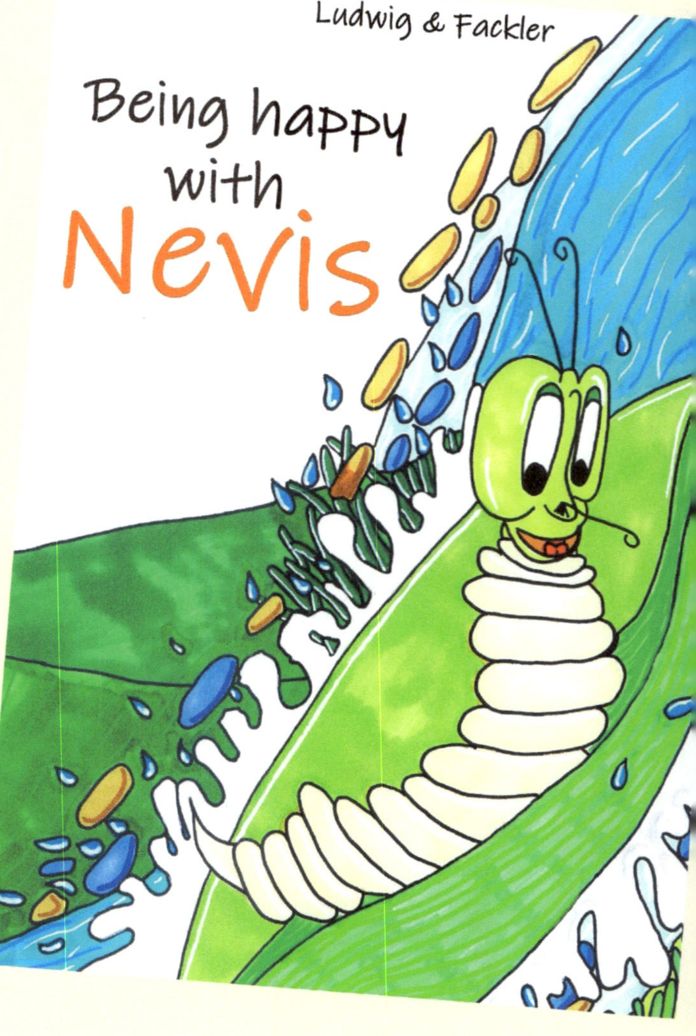

Painting Black

On a desk, there is Ruler who, by nature, wants to draw straight lines. Triangle wants to measure angles. While Pencil, meant for math, actually wants to create a children's book. The crayons, however, want nothing to do with a pencil that is yellow on the outside and grey on the inside'. Eraser usually just wants to rest, because her work would wear her down.

Painting Black tells the story of the creation of a children's book and explains that everyone has their purpose and that cooperation is best for everyone. In the process, the stationery utensils are brought to life and given personalities to make both the children and adult readers giggle.
Who knew Crayons squeak while painting?

How do Dinosaurs Sleep?

"How do Dinosaurs Sleep?" is a short bedtime story about a young Triceratops. Little Cara can't sleep because her feet hurt from walking. To learn how other dinosaurs spend the night, the curious young dinosaur takes a nightly walk through the jungle.

On her route, Cara discovers some peculiarities that the scientists would never have suspected: cuddling Velociraptors, a Tyrannosaurus rex with a wooden dummy, a snoring Diplodocus and many more.
The narrative is embellished with uplifting illustrations designed to soothe the reader, make them smile and send them off for a good night's sleep. In addition, "How do Dinosaurs Sleep?" includes 24 drawings for colouring in.

The page with the empty frame can be printed at
www.C-L-LUDWIG.com
and pasted over the advertisement to create
additional space in Leo's gallery.

CPSIA information can be obtained
at www.ICGtesting.com
Printed in the USA
LVHW070446010422
714994LV00002B/44